Fantasy of Happiness

Kenny Burnett

BookLeaf
Publishing

India | USA | UK

Presentation by *BookLeaf Publishing*

Web: www.bookleafpub.com

E-mail: info@bookleafpub.com

ISBN: 9789357447508

First edition 2022

DEDICATION

I dedicate this book to my amazing, supportive uncles, John & Scott, and my wonderful fiancee, Beth. They gave me the strength to keep going, even when life seemed impossible.

ACKNOWLEDGEMENT

I would like to thank my fiancee, Beth for pushing me to write this book, even when I didn't believe I could do it. She kept me going until the last minute.

I would also like to thank my uncles, John & Scott for believing in me, and helping me through the hardest moments of my life.

Lastly, a big thank you to my friends, Danny and Lexie, who push me to take the time and consider what I need.

I don't know where I would be without any of you. I love you guys.

PREFACE

Throughout this book, there are many references to mental health and the reason behind the author's attitude towards controversial topics. This book is personal, and opens up about their reality.

This is not meant to be a breaking point, but a release on those toxic faults.

Straw Houses

Straw houses with beds of steel wool
Built on a cracked foundation
The winds of fate, violent and cool
It left me with a revelation

The first house stood with false confidence
Its tenants hiding behind masks
A giant's angry footsteps made them wince
And still no one asks

Shaking, sputtering, crying out
Fear had weaved itself into the walls
No one could care what it was about
When it fell, no one heard my calls

Straw houses never felt safe
Even when the walls were braided
Suddenly I believed I was a waif
All my dreams had faded

A second ticked by, a minute, an hour
Number two hung above the clouds
For a while this place had seemed like home, a
tower
It was not long before it became shroud

Secluded, deranged, obsessed with stress
Bugs crawled, infesting the roots
The second, a home, fell into distress
This time I ran away without boots

Straw houses were an imitation
But they lead me to believe
This is why when I had no limitation
I took my leave

Finally a house of stone
Where the walls would not bend to the wind
The cruel wolf would howl alone
The violence could rescind

Steel wool turned into armor
Straw remained in my mold
Now I know there is far more
The straw became my rope to hold

Support Systems

One, two, three, all systems go

Steam and sweat and tears spilling

Rusty gears start turning again

A simple tune up

Bringing the desolate back to life

One engineer on maintenance

Hands on, painted black

Two programmers fixing the file

Running through codes, weeding out bugs

Three workers stand by willing to lend
themselves

They give their hearts to the machine

A purring engine, and it swiftly moves

Taking the next first step

Hello Mary Sunshine

How did you wake so soon?

I was hoping you would stay

Dreaming on the moon

Where everything is cast away

Except for your imagination

How did you wake so soon?

Your open eyes are the last station

They never fail to make me swoon

I nudge you from your precious sleep

How did you wake so soon?

You know my soul is yours to keep

Take it before noon

How did you wake so soon?

Hello Mary Sunshine

Take your floating dreams and put them in a
balloon

You are now mine

Debris

I didn't know I was carrying it
Until I came home
The weight was crushing
So I loaded it on my shoulders
Lifted it to the top shelf
Shoved it as far back as I could

Box after box
Filled with different poisons
They began to corrode
Leaking onto the shelf
Mixing into a dangerous cocktail
Eventually, everything was infected

Memories melded with reality
Current pain matching with past
Expired sickness now revived
Bringing red to my eyes
Logic had no place
It all felt the same

When my sight cleared
Debris was all that remained
So I pulled out another box
And repeated my pattern

Gathering all the pieces
I didn't know the debris was killing me

I Am Not Broken

I am not broken
And was never yours to fix

You are the reason
I have a surrounding cast

Built from bloody iron
Collected from a dead shell

I had to re-build
And find what I was made of

I used old pieces
Suddenly, they did not fit

Adding them was wrong
Taking them out did not work

Instead they changed
Determination and work

I knew I would mend
If only I had the time

I am not broken
And was never yours to fix

Bi-Polar Disorder

She brings me calamity
And cleans up the mess

She makes me manic
And then depressed

She brings me joy
In disastrous quantities

And pulls me down
Into my grave

When she picks me up again
I wonder what game she's playing

Taking my sanity
And making it fake

Taking my joy
And trading it for dismay

I sometimes wonder
If I should learn to play

Night Drives

We look for the perfect spot

Where the stars shine

Without competition of the city lights

Gleaming through artificial casings

Our spot is out there

And she wants to see the sky

Glistening like diamonds

We swarm to them

Like bees to honey

If I could I'd gather them

And keep them in a jar

The Wonderful Alice of Oz

What was in the tea?

Now all I can see

Is a cat with a grin

Leading me into a world of sin

The colours swirl

The teacups twirl

He leads me down a beaten path

While the witch waits in a bath

All her monkeys in a line

How will all of this turn out fine?

With ruby red heels

Caught up in ordeals

13

Am I a Writer?

There are days I wonder
If I'm supposed to be a writer
Sometimes I stare at a blank page
Waiting for the words to come
When they don't
I get defeated

Isn't writing supposed to be natural?
Isn't it supposed to be easy?
The daily grind of putting food on the table
Sucks inspiration like a siphon
The constant self-adorned pressure
Makes artistry impossible

Maybe if I had the time
To sit and ponder on a rhyme
My passion would grow back
I'd write about the little things
The joy I remember
Sitting in the leaves

Still I imagine a life
Dedicated to writing stories
Sharing tales with the world

Creating mountains out of ink
All the small things that life brings
Deserve their place on the page

If I am a writer
Things will turn out fine
I'll find the time
The small things that belong
Those fleeting moments of bliss
They deserve their place in imaginations

Reversed

To live without strife

I have never been so bold

I left my old life

Cocoon

When a caterpillar seals itself
In the folds of a cocoon
Does it know this is not the end?

When all the changes start to come
Modifying its balance
How is this not the end of the world?

Caterpillars never reach the finish line
They always need to transform
Does this seem fair?

Maybe the caterpillar knows
That this is only temporary
How would they though?

When I was a caterpillar
The world was dark
Does that pay the price for beauty?

Once my cocoon was ready
It took forever to go inside
How would I know I was ready?

It's Only Temporary

I hear the words more than I'd like

Everything takes time

This temporary feeling

Doesn't seem to be fleeting

Even though it shouldn't last

I can't see the end of the line

Days go on

Trudging through the trenches

Feeling the rain pour down

The fog thickens

I worry that temporary

Might be too long

Unwritten

My hands are bound
By relentless ropes

My head swims
With too many words

Instead of speaking them
I cry

The river overflows
Flooding the banks

Washing away the underbrush
Carrying waterlogged treasures

The babbling brook speaks for me
It is my scribe

Quiet murmurs layered
Many voices silently scream

Waiting for their moment
To finally be heard

Open Ended

I ask questions

And forget the subject

So the end is empty

Waiting to be finished

I can't think of the words

My mouth frozen in time

Tongue twisted

Straining to end

That's when she comes in

And catches the words

Left to hang

In a net

She takes the time

With understanding

To make sure it isn't

Left hanging

Bully

A single small push

Is multiplied by sundown

Was it deserved?

Medication

Once someone asked me

Do you want to live relying on pills?

And so I was determined

To find my own way out

When things got dark

My flashlight dimmed

The batteries grew weaker

Corroding

Still those words rang in my ear

I couldn't give in

And so I gave the light a shake

It flickered and stayed lit

Throughout the years

The glow faded

As the batteries eroded

But I had to be fine

I couldn't rely on medication

I had to find my own way out

Still, every time I built a ladder

The rungs came loose

Embarrassed by my failure

My inability to cope

I turned away a working light

Because it came with terms

Daily ingestion

Solitude ensuring privacy

I could never speak of what I took

Or how I got it

I was taught that pills

Were not the solution

So I turned them away

Sealing my own fate

Eventually my light went out

The corrosion had spread

Deteriorating what touched it

And so I accepted darkness

For a while things were calm

The dark wasn't so bad

Until all that came were thoughts

That dragged me to the ground

I felt defeated when I took the chance

To alter my imbalance

I was not good enough

To fix my own problems

Once I accepted

My head cleared

Though the light still flickered

It never went out again

Ponderosa

I have a dream

I named it Ponderosa

And though it is mine

I gave it no love

Ponderosa held my passions

The ones I had no time for

The ones I wished would come to life

By holding on too tightly

Ponderosa has many layers

But it is only a dream

Maybe if I wish hard enough

It'll be more to me

Failure Comes At A Price

Failure comes at a price
It isn't more than you can give

Knowledge gained and pride balance out
Teaching you how to live

If you think you're failing now
Wait until you come through the sieve

PTSD

My bomb is stomping footsteps
My minefield is the words I choose
The eggshells I walk around

My flashbacks are violent
With tendrils around my neck
Keeping the air from my lungs

The patterns are in solitude
Spending time alone
Without the comfort of a companion

My trenches are lined with crates
Stuffed with useless treasures
Hoarded and forgotten

The musky scent of mustard gas
Is covered by sickening florals
Melting on the floor

Damage prevention was my goal
Flipping the switch
So I didn't receive the strike I feared most

Institution

I remember the socks

They had little plastic grips

So no one would slip

I remember feeling insane

But it was contained

Inside pale green walls

I remember the loneliness

Until I found those who knew

What I felt was not a lie

I remember the food

Counting every bite

So I could eat what was gifted to me

I remember feeling better

Like life had a point

And I knew I had to leave

Kenny

Kept inside a box for so long

Everything seemed out of reach

New experiences brought me out

Nothing felt the same

Yet I pretended it was

Keeping secrets from those I cared about

Earning my silence

Neatly organising my thoughts

Not one was uncatalogued

Yesterday was a passing thought

Kindling for the fire

Eternally, I would be stronger

Nourishing the pale horse

Not ready to ride

Youth was still calling

www.ingramcontent.com/pod-product-compliance
Lightning Source LLC
La Vergne TN
LVHW051241200726
843510LV00011B/1643